Original title:
The Pollen Path

Copyright © 2025 Creative Arts Management OÜ
All rights reserved.

Author: Thomas Sinclair
ISBN HARDBACK: 978-1-80566-638-7
ISBN PAPERBACK: 978-1-80566-923-4

Whispers of Golden Dust

In the garden, bees take flight,
Wobbling left, then darting right.
A dance of joy, a sweet parade,
While flowers giggle in the shade.

With pollen shoes, they skip and hop,
From bloom to bloom, they never stop.
They wear their armor made of dust,
And taste the nectar, oh, they must!

Nectar's Journey

A bumblebee with grand ambition,
Embarked upon a sweet nutrition.
He spread his legs, not very sly,
And wore a crown of yellow high.

He flew too close to a garden hose,
And learned the truth that everyone knows.
When smelling flowers with delight,
Be wary of the spritz at night!

Blooming Memories

Remember when we took that trip,
To see the flowers—what a blip!
You sneezed and startled all the bees,
They buzzed away with such great ease.

With every bloom, we shared a laugh,
As petals tickled, oh what a gaffe!
A memory sweet, forever stored,
In the book of blooms we've adored.

Dance of the Honeybees

In fields of gold, a ball they throw,
With wiggly tails and quite a show.
They twirl and spin, such charming fools,
The checkered dance floor, nature's schools.

They sip the sugar, feeling bold,
Trading tales of nectar gold.
With every buzz a story grows,
In the hive where laughter flows!

Sweet Serenade of Spring

Bees buzz loudly, full of cheer,
While flowers dance, month's debut here.
A dandelion's wish flies with glee,
As I dodge sprinkles from a bumblebee.

The sun's a joker, playing tricks,
Warming up all those floral flicks.
Tulips are flaunting their bright attire,
And squirrels prance in a nature choir.

Beneath the Swaying Blossoms

Under blooms that tickle the sky,
A sneezing fit makes me sigh.
Petals rain like confetti bright,
While I chase shadows, laughing in flight.

Butterflies flit with a flappy toast,
As I ponder which flower I like most.
A squirrel steals my cookie crumb,
While bees just hover, drumming a thrum.

A Tapestry of Tiny Wings

A hummingbird zooms with a peek-a-boo,
While ladybugs march in a conga line too.
The caterpillar tells a joke so slow,
And starts to giggle, 'Look at me grow!'

A dance-off among the blossoms unfolds,
As ants in tuxedos share chocolate molds.
With laughter loud, the breezes play,
In this garden comedy, we'll sway.

The Alchemy of Life

In spring's lab, potions of bloom,
Mix giggles with pollen, dispelling the gloom.
Laughter bubbles, rising like dough,
With every tickle from a butterfly's toe.

Rabbits plan pranks, hopping in style,
While bees don glasses, staying a while.
Life's silly recipes stir joy like cake,
Baking smiles in every mistake.

Chasing the Honeyed Melodies

Buzzing bees sing high and low,
Their little dance puts on a show.
With sticky feet they hop and jive,
Turning flowers bright and alive.

Collecting sweetness, they can't resist,
To leave a trail on a nectar quest.
Winging wildly, they twirl and spin,
In the great race, let the laughter begin!

Where Colors Meet the Sky

Up above, shades try to play,
Mixing blue and pink all day.
Dandelions chase the sun,
In this garden, everyone's having fun!

A butterfly floats with flair so neat,
Trying to dance on the dog's big feet.
The flowers giggle in a sunny clump,
As the bees buzz by with a happy thump.

Echoes of Floral Delight

Petals whisper secrets sweet,
As bunnies hop and tiny feet meet.
Fragrant laughs fill the bubbling air,
While ladybugs wiggle without a care.

In this realm where joy abounds,
Silly squirrels sprint round and round.
The flowers sway, wearing a grin,
Join the chorus, let the fun begin!

Pathways of Flourishing Hues

In a world of colors, bright and bold,
Tales of petals, funny and told.
A flower fell, in a tumble, blight,
Yet it giggled, 'I'll stand upright!'

The sunflowers wave their golden heads,
As squirrels prance on their fluffy beds.
Each stem shimmies in the warm spring breeze,
Celebrating the joy with such ease!

Fragrance of a New Dawn

Morning wakes with a giggle,
Birds in tights start to wiggle.
Flowers burst with colors bright,
Dancing bees in pure delight.

Sunbeams slip, play hide and seek,
While ants march, a tiny clique.
Each petal holds a funny trick,
Nature's jest, a joyful flick.

Breeze whispers secrets, oh so sly,
Telling tales of clouds that fly.
Daisy chains with laughter made,
In the sun, shadows parade.

Laughter echoes through the sky,
Honey drops, oh me, oh my!
A new dawn brings a hum and dance,
In this world, we spin and prance.

Beneath the Veil of Petals

Underneath a curtain soft,
Bumblebees pollinate aloft.
Petals chuckle as they sway,
Surely bloom is here to play.

Ladybugs in stylish wear,
Strutting 'round without a care.
Whispers float from leaf to leaf,
Plant jokes bring such sweet relief.

Butterflies in comic shoes,
Flutter by with giggly cues.
Beneath each petal's grand display,
Life is but a vibrant play.

In this garden, joy's the theme,
Nature croons a playful dream!
Sing along in colorful charms,
Underneath where laughter warms.

A Journey Through Golden Haze

Golden rays with sparks of cheer,
Sunflowers nod, 'We're glad you're here!'
Wandering through this vibrant maze,
Finding gags in every gaze.

Fluttering flaps of a silly crow,
Mimicking dances, putting on a show.
Each twist and turn's a funny sight,
In nature's laughter, pure delight.

Breezy whispers, tickle the grass,
While clovers dance with such a sass.
Every step in this sunlit place,
Laughter blooms, a cheerful grace.

In the haze, where giggles roam,
Every flower feels like home.
In this land of fun and light,
Mirth and joy take joyous flight.

Secrets of the Blooming Meadow

In the meadow, secrets creep,
With flowers at their giggling peep.
Each bud tells a funny tale,
While frogs in tuxedos set to sail.

Dandelions puff like clowns,
Blowing wishes all around.
While bunnies hop with silly grace,
Wearing hats that match their face.

Grass blades tease the passing breeze,
Catching whispers with such ease.
A tapestry of jokes unfolds,
In every petal that it holds.

So join the party, laugh and play,
In this bloom where jesters stay.
Secrets sprout where humor thrives,
In a meadow where joy arrives.

Lullabies on a Breezy Day

Tiny bees parade along,
While flowers dance to nature's song.
Breezes tickle with a sigh,
As petals wave and butterflies fly.

Silly squirrels hop and prance,
Their furry tails in a springtime dance.
Giggling daisies sway in sun,
Where nature's laughter's just begun.

The air is sweet with fragrant cheer,
And every giggle brings good cheer.
A breeze whispers to the bloom,
As flowers giggle, dispelling gloom.

Joyful whispers fill the air,
Playing tag without a care.
On this day of sunny glee,
All is bright as it can be.

Glimpses of Hidden Wonder

Underneath the leafy shade,
A hidden dance, a vibrant parade.
Mice in tuxedos take their chance,
While fireflies join the wiggly dance.

Wobbly worms in slack-lined shoes,
Twirl and spin with nothing to lose.
A ladybug plays peek-a-boo,
Tickling the leaves as it flits through.

Whimsical frogs croak out a tune,
While frogs in hats chase the moon.
In this world of silly sights,
Even shadows giggle in the lights.

Oh what fun, this day's delight,
With nature laughing, oh so bright.
Every creature, great and small,
Participates in this grand ball.

In the Realm of Blossoming Hues

Colors burst in bright array,
Painting smiles along the way.
Tulips wear their polka dots,
While violets play with funny spots.

Sunflowers stretch, necks so tall,
Tip their hats at butterflies small.
Dandelions play hide-and-seek,
With giggles echoing down the creek.

Jellybean clouds roll on by,
As bees spin yarns with a sigh.
Who knew blooms could be so zany,
In this garden, life is crazy!

From blushing buds to wild greens,
The joy of spring is rarely seen.
In this realm where laughter coos,
Everything's bright in blossoming hues.

Sweet Traces of Seasonal Change

When spring bursts forth with colors bright,
Cartwheeling critters feel just right.
Chirping birds in silly hats,
Dancing leaves and playful chats.

Swaying branches join the fun,
While puddles splash in bright-eyed run.
Bumblebees in yellow stripes,
Form a band with nature's types.

Each flower shares a wink and grin,
As giggles sprinkle on the wind.
Oh how the season spins and twirls,
In a dance that makes the heart hurl.

From the sun to the moonlight's glow,
Every corner holds a show.
The sweet traces of life's delight,
Bring joy to hearts, day and night.

Journeying through Soft Shadows

In fields of flowers, I start my quest,
Dodging bees, I give my best.
A clumsy tumble, oh what a sight,
Pollen on my nose, it feels just right.

A path of yellow, a splash of green,
Smiling daisies are quite the scene.
I sneeze and giggle, oh what a mess,
Nature's party? I must confess!

With sticky fingers and pollen-laden hair,
I dance like no one else is there.
A butterfly laughs, it flutters by,
"Come join the fun!" it seems to cry.

With each new step, I hum a tune,
While bees and blooms make me swoon.
This joyful promenade, an endless spree,
I'd trade my shoes for honey, you see!

A Canvas of Nature's Tapestry

On this canvas, hues collide,
Where colors mix, and whims abide.
A brush of bees, a splash of cheer,
The artist waits — it's finally here!

Petals kick up as I skip along,
With every misstep, I sing a song.
Pollinated giggles in the air,
Nature's brush with flair to spare.

A painter's palette, vibrant, bold,
With laughter, stories never told.
I slip on dew, oh what a scene,
I'll make it work, just like a dream!

The canvas shifts with every breeze,
Tickled grass tickles my knees.
In this wild art, I take my stand,
With nature's brush in clumsy hand!

Dreamscapes of Color and Life

In dreamscapes bright, what do I see?
A world of giggles, buzzing free.
Colors bouncing, a wild delight,
Swirling pigments in morning light.

The flowers dance, a vibrant show,
Tickling toes where the breezes flow.
I wiggle and jiggle, caught in a daze,
Lost in the laughter of summer's haze.

A ladybug slides with style so grand,
While I trip over my own two hands.
"More nectar, please!" I shout in glee,
As blooms unleash their humor at me.

In this dreamscape, I spin and sway,
With colors and laughter, I'll play all day.
A canvas where joy is in bloom,
This world of whimsy makes my heart zoom!

Garden's Gentle Breath

Bumblebees dance in a wobbly way,
Chasing the flowers that won't stay.
Sunsets giggle in shades of gold,
As daisies whisper secrets untold.

Mud pies crumble with laughter and cheer,
While butterflies flutter without a fear.
Worms tell jokes beneath the ground,
Each chuckle a treasure waiting to be found.

Secrets of the Sunlit Field

A snail in sunglasses browses the grass,
Taking its time, like a slow-moving class.
Crickets tune-up for a grand night show,
While fireflies twinkle, putting on a glow.

Ants hold a meeting, discussing the crumbs,
While a butterfly giggles, it dances and hums.
The sun winks down, a mischievous star,
In the field of secrets, where laughter's not far.

Fluttering Footprints

A tiny frog hops in big green boots,
Waving at squirrels dressed up as hoots.
The trail of petals, a colorful mess,
Leaves laughter echoing, couldn't care less.

Chasing the shadows as they prance,
Each footprint a story, each leap a dance.
Ladybugs giggle, tickling the air,
In this silly world, joy's always there.

Symphony of the Senses

Whiffs of mint tickle the nose,
As goofy raccoons put on their clothes.
Sights of bright blooms, a patchwork quilt,
Make the garden burst with a rainbow built.

The sounds of crunching beneath little feet,
As squirrels play tag in a comical feat.
Taste the honey dripped sweet like a dream,
In this whimsical world, fun reigns supreme.

The Language of Petal and Wing

Bees wear tuxedos, buzz on parade,
Chatting with lilies, sipping sweet aid.
While butterflies waltz, in colors they flare,
Roses roll their eyes, pretending not to care.

Grasshoppers tap dance, with legs like a pro,
Crickets join in, putting on quite a show.
Under the sun's lens, all gather to sing,
Nature's own soap opera, on fluttering wing.

Radiance in Every Falling Grain

Seeds on a quest, they fall from the sky,
Like confetti at parties, oh my, oh my!
Dandelions giggle, as they take a flight,
Spreading their laughter, from morning to night.

Sunflowers draw faces, with wide, silly grins,
They chase after clouds, they dare them to spin.
In fields of delight, they play tag with the breeze,
Planting their joy with whimsical ease.

The Harmony of Nature's Secrets

Frogs croak karaoke, under the moonlight,
While fireflies twinkle, they're stars taking flight.
Nature's a jester, with tricks up her sleeve,
A symphony of laughter, if you just believe.

Worms in their burrows play hide-and-seek,
Finding their way, with their squiggly streak.
Ladybugs gossip, perched high on a leaf,
Sharing the news of each happy belief.

Fragrant Journeys in Stillness

Flowers in silence, hold secrets galore,
Whispers of nectar, they want to explore.
Ants form a parade, with snacks in their grasp,
While petals are plotting a gentle sweet gasp.

Clouds wander lazy, casting shadows of fun,
Sprinkling a giggle, from each little run.
In this quirky garden, where antics are true,
Every petal and wing has a tale to construe.

Dance of Dusty Motifs

In the air, they swirl and twine,
Tiny flecks, a ballet divine.
Sneezing fits as they ascend,
Nature's confetti, our playful friend.

Chasing them like children play,
Whirling dervishes on a sunny day.
Laughter echoes in the breeze,
As pollen teases with such ease.

Wrinkled noses, a comical sight,
Eyes so red in the golden light.
We giggle through a fragrant haze,
Caught in nature's silly maze.

So let's twirl with buds and bees,
A waltz of wonder, if you please.
A dance of dust beneath the sun,
Where every jest has just begun.

Blossoms on the Wind

Blossoms flutter, a cheeky flight,
Twirling petals in pure delight.
They tickle noses, play hide and seek,
With every sneeze, we laugh and squeak.

Sticky fingers from a wild chase,
Nature's pranksters in every place.
The wind giggles, sends them high,
Fashion statements for each passerby.

Allergies dance with a playful grin,
Silly faces as they zoom in.
With pollen miracles in the air,
It's a funny world, beyond compare.

So let's run wild, hearts in sync,
With blossoms giggling, don't you think?
A merry jest by Mother Nature,
Life's a comedy, and it's our wager.

Sweet Stains of Morning Light

Morning sun spills its bright cheer,
Carrying whispers that tickle near.
Stains of gold on grassy plains,
Chasing shadows as daylight gains.

Sneezes mix with laughter's sound,
As blossoms tumble to the ground.
Ticklish scents weave through the day,
A sweet perfume in a playful play.

Bumblebees join the merry fray,
Buzzing jokes, come what may.
With every swish, and every flop,
Nature's giggle never stops.

So let's savor this fleeting grace,
Giddy moments we won't replace.
For every pollen puff that flies,
Is laughter hidden in disguise.

Fluttering Dreams and Sunlight

Fluttering dreams on rays of gold,
Whimsical tales of the bold.
They dash and dart, a sneaky crew,
Little jesters in skies so blue.

Sunlight spills where the shadows play,
Tickled by pollen in a funny way.
Floating whispers with a silly jest,
Making our shadows laugh the best.

Sneezing fits and giggling sounds,
Nature's comedy in leaps and bounds.
With every flutter, let spirits soar,
Chasing dreams from shore to shore.

So let's skip beneath this hue,
Making memories, just me and you.
In the dance of fluff and delight,
Life's a punchline, always bright.

The Journey of Sipping Bees

Buzzing on a wild quest,
Dancing with each flower's jest.
A sip of nectar, oh so sweet,
Who knew adventure could taste like a treat?

Flipping and flopping, watch them go,
Sticky with pollen, putting on a show.
They giggle as they change course,
Following scents with no remorse.

Sunshine winks upon their flight,
They laugh at petals, pure delight.
"Is that a tulip or a giant cake?"
They murmur softly, for goodness' sake!

In the end, with buzzes bright,
They share their tales and take to night.
The buzzing chorus sings their praise,
For sipping bees in sunny days.

Flickering Light in Bloom

Amidst the buds, a glow appears,
Fluttering sparks dance through the years.
Each bloom a lantern, quirky and bright,
Guiding a party of giddy delight.

A daisy slips, a tulip trips,
Laughing in chorus, no one skips.
Petal siblings sway and tease,
"Oh look, I'm a butterfly!" with ease.

Wiggling roots call out for fun,
"Join us, here, everyone!"
In the spark of twilight's charm,
Every flower shoots a smile, no harm.

The evening's glow grows wide and deep,
As flowers giggle, the secrets they keep.
With flickering joy in every bloom,
They frolic beneath the silvery moon.

Swaying Through a Meadow's Embrace

In the meadow where the grasses sway,
Nature hosts a lively play.
Butterflies waltz, in a grand old dance,
While bees tell jokes, a flowery romance.

"Why did the flower break up?" they tease,
"It found a weed that wouldn't leave!"
With every buzz, the jokes take flight,
Petal giggles echo through the night.

Dandelions puff out whispers so sly,
"You'll never believe what I saw fly by!"
Each seed a traveler, ready to roam,
Swaying together, they feel at home.

As twilight paints the sky aglow,
The meadow hums, with laughter it flows.
In this embrace of joy and cheer,
Life's simple pleasures bring us near.

Petal-Wrapped Memories

Once upon a time, in a garden fair,
Memories bloomed in fragrant air.
A daisy's whisper, a tulip's wink,
Caught in laughter before we think.

Petals wrapped like silly gifts,
Storing moments with joyful lifts.
"Remember when the rain wore shoes?
We danced around, singing our blues!"

A blossom beams, "I've tales to share,
Of sun and shade, of love and care."
With every wind, the stories twirl,
Petal-wrapped secrets begin to unfurl.

In this garden of laughter and glee,
We find joy in the smallest spree.
Memories bloom under skies up high,
In a petal-wrapped world, we all fly.

Interludes in Blooming Fields

In the field where daisies dance,
Bees try their sweet romance.
Each flower wears a jolly hat,
Pollens swirling, just like that!

A dandelion sneezes loud,
Joining in with all the crowd.
Tulips giggle in the sun,
Nature's joke has just begun!

Butterflies on secret quests,
Try to blend in with their vests.
But oh, a wink from ladybug,
Spills the beans, what a snug hug!

As sunbeams join the playful spree,
Frogs leap high, a sight to see.
In this bloom of sweet delight,
Nature's laughter takes to flight!

Whispered Colors in Harmony

Roses blush in shades of sly,
While lilacs whisper, 'Oh my, my!'
A bumblebee hums a tune,
Buzzing 'neath the friendly moon.

Sunflowers pondering their height,
Ask the clouds, 'Is this alright?'
With a wink, they tilt their heads,
Making friends where laughter spreads.

Jasmine's scent has tales to tell,
Of frogs in suits who sing so well.
Petals prance like lively sprites,
Colors twirl in silly flights!

Every hue is in a race,
To see who can make the best face.
A riot of shades, a comic scene,
Nature's jesters, bright and keen!

Echoing Moments of Enchantment

In gardens lush, a sly old cat,
Finds shadows from a friendly rat.
They share secrets of the flower,
How to nap at spring's fine hour!

Breezes giggle, rustling trees,
Tickling leaves like playful bees.
A snail boasts of his great pace,
While daisies bloom in silly grace.

Chirping birds, a choir tease,
Sing of nectar and of bees.
With every note, a sprout will sway,
Joining in their merry play.

Mushrooms giggle in their rows,
Pausing as a garden grows.
Nature's stage, where all partake,
Echoes of joy, no mistake!

Murmurs of the Spring Breeze

A wind that whispers through the grass,
Tells stories of each lovely lass.
Pansies gossip all day long,
While doves coo a soft love song.

Caterpillars wear their ties,
Gazing up at sunny skies.
Chasing dreams of flying high,
They munch on leaves while passing by.

A curious cloud drifts overhead,
Dropping laughs where flowers spread.
With every drop, a joke is made,
Nature's fun, in sunshine laid.

With croaks and chirps the chorus grows,
In celebration, anything goes!
Spring's delight, so wild and free,
A merry, blooming jubilee!

Garden of Whispered Wishes

In the garden where gnomes snicker,
Bumblebees dance with a silly flicker.
Dandelions blow, wishing they could fly,
While crickets chirp, "Oh me, oh my!"

Sunflowers shake in the gentle breeze,
With secrets shared among the trees.
Mice play tag with a cheeky grin,
As earthworms giggle, "Let the fun begin!"

Digging deep for a treasure chest,
Only to find a garden pest!
Plants chuckle, "Here comes another bug,!"
As they all snuggle, feeling snug.

With every bloom, a laugh takes flight,
In the garden's joyful, silly light.
Watch flowers sway, with chuckles so sweet,
In this whimsical place, life's a treat!

Tapestry of a Vibrant Season

Colors burst like a party loud,
While leaves twirl, oh how they proud!
Butterflies sip on sweet nectar fun,
While daisies join in the silly run.

The bees bring tunes, a buzz so bright,
Making flowers dance with sheer delight.
Frogs croak jokes by the bubbling brook,
While the sun glances with a cheeky look.

Caterpillars munch with tiny giggles,
While the wind jives, shaking all wiggly wiggles.
As clouds float by in cotton-candy hues,
Rainbows appear, sharing colorful news!

Every petal sings a funny song,
In the tapestry, where all belong.
Nature's jesters in a vibrant show,
A playful cycle, giving us glow!

Scent of the Whispering Woods

In the woods where shadows play,
Squirrels gossip about their day.
Mushrooms wink as rabbits hop,
With every step, the laughter pops!

Trees tell tales of wise old birds,
Cracking jokes without any words.
A bear snorts as he finds a snack,
While the deer dance, giving no slack!

Mossy carpets softly creak,
As chipmunks make a giggly cheek.
Forget-me-nots whisper in the air,
While the breeze tickles without a care.

In this place of joy and cheer,
Nature's humor draws us near.
With every rustle, there's something new,
In the woods where laughter grew!

Harmonies of Nature's Heart

In the meadow where the daisies sway,
Frogs compose their silly ballet.
Birds chirp tunes on a sunny stage,
While squirrels jot down their funny page.

Buttercups twinkle with youthful cheer,
As butterflies giggle, "Come look here!"
Grasshoppers leap to a wild beat,
Creating rhythms beneath our feet.

The sun winks down with a sly smile,
As flowers chat in their own style.
Petals fall like confetti galore,
Celebrating life, forever more!

In this dance of colors and light,
Nature's heart sings with sheer delight.
Join the fun, and let laughter ring,
In this harmony, where joy takes wing!

The Music of Fluttering Wings

In the garden where bees buzz loud,
A butterfly sings, oh, so proud.
It flutters here, it flutters there,
With polka-dot wings and flowing hair.

Grasshoppers join in the wild spree,
While ants march on, so orderly.
They've got their own little jiving crew,
Who knew that bugs could be so shrewd?

A ladybug hails from her leaf throne,
Claiming this patch as her own zone.
With tiny glasses and a sly smile,
She plans to party in style for a while.

The crickets cook up a late-night feast,
While fireflies illuminate, to say the least.
What a ruckus, what a show,
Insects have got it, oh don't you know!

A Dance Among the Blossoms

In a world where flowers wear bright hats,
Daisies prance while dodging the bats.
Roses twist and twirl with flair,
Iris leaps with delicate care.

The sunflowers stretch, waving arms so long,
While daisies be bop to the buzz of a song.
Tulips jump in a line, oh so neat,
It's a floral rave, get on your feet!

Butterflies float, with grace they soar,
As petals party on the lush green floor.
Colorful fun in a petal parade,
With pollen confetti, plans are laid.

The lilacs giggle, smelling so sweet,
As bees join the fun, they can't take a seat.
In this wacky waltz of bloom and wing,
Nature's ballet is the silliest thing!

Threads of Flora's Song

In the meadow where the daisies weave,
Silly songs that you wouldn't believe.
A dandelion winks with a puff so round,
As wildflowers giggle and dance from the ground.

Oh, the violets joke about their hue,
While tulips tease in red and blue.
The sun tickles petals, making them sing,
In this fabric of fun, joy's the only king.

A spider spins webs, a narrative grand,
Catching the laughter with a silky strand.
Each bloom echoes with pollen delight,
In this frolicsome place, from morning till night.

When twilight glows and stars appear,
Flora's choir sings just for you to hear.
Join in the chorus of cheery cheer,
In this bustling garden, let's spread the cheer!

Boughs Beneath the Golden Glow

Under the trees, where the fruit hangs low,
Squirrels play tag with a cheeky crow.
They tumble and bounce in the summer's heat,
While shadows dance around their feet.

The apples giggle as the birds take flight,
Claiming their shade in the warm sunlight.
While branches sway, the breeze does twirl,
It's a treehouse party in a leafy whirl.

Bees bring the snacks from flower to leaf,
While butterflies dream of fancy belief.
"Let's squeeze the juice out of sunny days,"
Said the green grapes, in laughter they sway.

As dusk rolls in with a golden hue,
Fireflies blink like stars breaking through.
Under the boughs, let laughter flow,
In this hilarious orchard, let good times grow!

Echoes of the Blooms

In the garden, bees do dance,
Buzzing loud, they take their chance.
Trying hard to steal the show,
But tripping on a flower, oh no!

Petals giggle in the breeze,
Watching bees drop to their knees.
"Hey there, guys, just take a seat,
You're stepping on my lovely feet!"

Under the Gilded Canopy

There's a squirrel, quite the prude,
With a stash of nuts, he's feeling shrewd.
He tries to climb the leafy stacks,
But ends up falling on his backs!

Sunbeams shine with cheeky flair,
As a ladybug twirls through the air.
"I'm a superstar!" she claims with pride,
While awkward ants continue to glide.

Heartbeats in the Meadow

Frogs are croaking, what a song!
As crickets chirp, it won't be long.
A rabbit hops, all filled with cheer,
But lands on a snail—oh dear!

A butterfly flutters, charming and bright,
"Why do you hop? Stick to flight!"
The rabbit shrugs, with a smirk so sly,
"I eat carrots, you just pass by!"

Flavors of the Breeze

In the air, the aromas clash,
Lemonade's sweet, but oh what a splash!
A careless kid with a cup in hand,
Turns a picnic into a sticky land!

The wind tickles flowers, they giggle and sway,
While clouds above mope in shades of gray.
"Oh come on, lighten up a bit!"
But they just rumble—what a funny fit!

Skies Over the Garden

In skies so blue, the bees do zoom,
With honey hats, they dance and bloom.
A rogue wasp steals a bit of sweet,
While ladybugs groan at the heat.

The daisies giggle, the tulips grin,
As ants march on, ready to win.
A squirrel takes a hop, then a leap,
In search of nuts, in a garden heap.

The sun's too hot, they need a shade,
A conga line of bugs is made.
Oh, what a scene in the backyard,
Where laughter's more than just a bard!

But watch out for splashes from the hose,
It's water games where everyone knows.
For in this funny floral show,
The wildest weeds put on a glow.

Fluttering Dreams of Spring

A butterfly with stripes so bold,
Wears shades of blue, if truth be told.
He flits and flutters, in search of fun,
While bumblebees hum, 'Hey, you've won!'

Dandelions puff, and seeds take flight,
While weeds protest, 'We're taking a bite!'
A grasshopper jumps, does a little dance,
While caterpillars form a marching prance.

The sun shines bright, the weather's neat,
As flowers pull pranks, oh what a feat!
Who ate my petals? They giggle and tease,
As petals rain down with the slightest breeze.

So poke your nose into this bloom,
Where giggles sprinkle, chase away gloom.
For laughter hides in petals so bright,
In this wacky world of day and night.

Whispers of Spring's Caress

In the garden, whispers float so free,
A snail suggests, 'Have tea with me!'
The sun shines down on a thistle's tale,
As worms play cards within the pale.

Bumblebees sport fancy galas anew,
While ants debate who's the best in blue.
A clumsy frog slips into the scene,
Making a splash like a quirky machine.

Tulips gossip in colors so bold,
With pots of soil that warm in the cold.
The bees wear crowns, the butterflies search,
For nectar's hottest springtime perch.

So gather round for tales of bright,
Where daisies sing till the falling night.
In every petal, a secret's told,
Of springtime's laughter, a joy to behold.

Nectar Trails of the Heart

In search of sweet, the bees do race,
Their sticky dance is quite the grace.
A dandelion shouts, 'Look at me!'
While the bumblebees buzz endlessly.

A ladybug with a hat so fine,
Claims ownership of the vine on vine.
The blooms rejoice as raindrops play,
Turning the garden into a cabaret.

The tulips argue on who's the best,
While oak trees sigh, taking a rest.
A squirrel performs balancing acts,
With acorns tucked in mysterious stacks.

Oh, nature's heart is a giggling spree,
With silly games for you and me.
In every petal, a chuckle lies,
A carnival of joy beneath the skies.

Golden Dust and Gentle Breezes

In the meadow, flowers laugh,
Bees in bow ties zoom and chaff.
They dance a jig, a sweet ballet,
While butterflies shout, 'Hip-hip-hooray!'

Golden dust floats in the air,
Sneezy sneezes everywhere!
With a tickle and a giggle cheer,
We all run fast, oh dear, oh dear!

Laughter blooms in every nook,
As bumblebees sip from the brook.
They hold a party, all aglow,
With honey cakes and tasty dough!

And nature pans a comic spree,
While daisies try to tease a bee.
"Oh darling, come on, join the fun!"
But bees just buzz and say, "We're done!"

Constellations in Pollinated Air

The flowers wink, they gleam at night,
As fireflies join the silly flight.
Stars above, with envy glare,
"Why can't we dance in fragrant air?"

The pollen grains float like dreams,
Tickling noses, bursting seams.
Ants in top hats march with style,
As ladybugs laugh and get all the smiles.

Bumblebees boast of their sweet fame,
While howling cats whisper a name.
"Who knew this life could be so grand?"
The flowers giggle, lending a hand!

Together they twirl, nature's jest,
From bloom to bloom, it's quite the quest.
In vibrant chats, they fill the air,
A cosmic giggle beyond compare!

Nature's Tender Embrace

With gentle hugs from sunbeams bright,
The daisies prank the poor old kite.
"Oh look at me, I'm flying high!"
But tangled strings make it cry!

Nature's fun has rhymes so sweet,
As squirrels play hide and seek at our feet.
Humble daisies give a shout,
"Join our game, we know the route!"

The ladybugs parade with flair,
Strutting like they just don't care.
"Catch us if you can," they plead,
As they frolic, that's guaranteed!

And as the sun dips in the west,
The flowers grin, "We're truly blessed.
To share in laughter, in this place,
Oh what fun, this tender space!"

The Breath of Flora's Dance

In gardens bright, giggles abound,
While tulips whisper without a sound.
The violets boast of their sweet scent,
As bees buzz by, so wildly bent.

With every sway, petals poke fun,
As clovers shout, "Let's skip and run!"
The breeze throws a ticklish dart,
While dandelions play their part.

Sunflowers giggle, tall and proud,
Waving hello to the giggling crowd.
"Hey there, friends, join in the whirl,
No frowns allowed, come give a twirl!"

A world of cheer, in colors bright,
Nature's ballet, a vivid sight.
In every hop and playful glance,
We find ourselves in Flora's dance!

Sunshine's Embrace

In the garden, bees are buzzing,
Flowers dance, while I'm just puzzling.
A butterfly sips from a bright bloom,
I trip and almost meet my doom.

Laughter echoes, the birds are all in,
Chasing shadows, it's where we begin.
My hat flies off, chasing the breeze,
While squirrels scamper, at ease with ease.

Sunshine laughs, a bright golden grin,
Nature's parade, we're all jumping in.
I drop my sandwich, oh what a scene,
A raiding raccoon, so crafty and keen.

Mosaic of Colors

A riot of colors, splashed everywhere,
Yellow sunflowers, no time to spare.
Petunias giggle in various hues,
While I stand here, choosing my shoes.

Dandelions puff, their wishes take flight,
I blow one away—was that wrong or right?
The bumblebees work, quite the busy crew,
While I ponder if I need a new shoe.

The flowers spark joy, a bright quilt in bloom,
I break into dance, oh, what a costume!
A ladybug lands, with a nod from the sky,
It seems to agree that I'm a bit spry.

Whirlwind of Whispers

A gust of wind tickles my ear,
Is that a secret I'm meant to hear?
Grasshoppers leap with a cheeky plan,
They chit and chat like a busy clan.

Leaves gossip softly, swaying and spry,
While the ants march on like a parade marching by.
I swing my arms, trying to catch fun,
Oh look, there goes still another run!

The whispers invite me to join the spree,
Nature's own jesters, come dance wild and free.
I stumble and spin, what a sight to behold,
Each twist and turn gives a giggle untold.

Transitory Delights

A moment in time—oh, what a feast,
With petals of sweetness, joy's little beast.
The breeze flips my pages with playful insistence,
While I sip lemonade, feeling its brilliance.

Clouds march in, wearing shadows of gray,
I race them in laughter, come join the play!
A tickle from daisies, a contented sigh,
With hiccups from laughter, how the time flies by.

As colors fade softly into the night,
Fireflies blink on, twinkling with light.
Tomorrow will bring a fresh set of quirks,
For life's little moments are where fun lurks!

The Essence of Flowering Adventures

In gardens full of buzzing bees,
A dandelion sneezes with ease.
Petals dance like silly geese,
Chasing dreams of a tasty feast.

The roses wear their finest hats,
While daisies gossip with the cats.
A bumblebee does acrobats,
Flipping past the chubby bats.

Sunflowers sway in the warm embrace,
While butterflies twirl in a race.
They laugh as if it's a silly chase,
Winks and giggles light up the space.

Amidst the blooms, a clamorous crew,
Hopping about, like they always do.
With pollen pockets, they paint the view,
A comedy show where all's askew.

Serendipity on Floral Routes

Through fields where flowers spin and twirl,
Bees trade tales with a laughing squirrel.
Each petal tells a secret whirl,
As stinging nettles plot and hurl.

The tulips giggle, colors bright,
While ladybugs dress for the night.
A snail in shades tries to take flight,
But ends up snoring, what a sight!

Orchids put on a masquerade,
With bees as dancers, unafraid.
Buzzing and flitting, they invade,
Creating chaos, the best charade.

At sunset's blush, they toast with cheer,
To every silly, buzzing peer.
Life's a garden; let's make it clear,
A party waits for those who dare!

Beneath the Blossoms' Glow

Underneath the petals' glimmer,
A cricket orchestrates a stammer.
Frogs croak jokes that make them shimmer,
As fluttering moths play the skimmer.

The fragrant breeze begins to tease,
With ticklish whispers through the trees.
A beetle struts, dressed to appease,
While flowers giggle in the breeze.

Jasmine plays hide-and-seek at dusk,
While munching ants debate and fuss.
Their tiny plans can't help but rust,
But every bloom joins in, they must!

Frolicsome moments, potion rich,
A symphony of fun, without a hitch.
So come and join—scratch that itch,
Life's a garden, switch by switch.

Pathway of Winged Companions

On a scenic route of color bright,
Birds sing confessions, full of delight.
A butterfly wonders, "Is it night?"
While bees buzz strategy for flight.

Petals gossip, petals strut,
A grasshopper jumps into a rut.
Dandelion fluff got a big cut,
As flower friends say, "What the…?"

Hummingbirds race, sipping with flair,
While caterpillars plot and stare.
With pollen snacks beyond compare,
They laugh until they lose their care.

In this whimsical floral scene,
Every path is fun and keen.
With each friend met, a new routine,
Life's an adventure, pure and serene!

The Nectar Seekers

Bee in a hurry, buzz like a car,
Chasing sweet spots, yes, that's the star.
Flutter and hover, the dance begins,
Sipping the blossoms, let's see who wins.

Ants in a line, what a sight to see,
On a crumb trail, a feast for a spree.
"Hey, wait for me!" shouts a forgetful mate,
But crumbs disappear, oh, isn't that fate?

Fluttering fairies, with faces so bright,
Stealing some nectar in the warm light.
Giggling loud as they stumble and fall,
"Who knew these daisies would cause such a brawl?"

With every drop, they skip and they hop,
Nature's circus, with no sign to stop.
"Did you try orange? It's pure liquid fun!"
Sipping and laughing, till day is all done.

Interlude of the Insects

A ladybug's got a spotty little game,
"Look at me shine!" oh, isn't she lame?
Caterpillar's munching, on leaves with delight,
"Just wait till I'm a butterfly, take flight!"

The grasshoppers sing, with legs like a flute,
"Hop to it folks, we'll dance to this tune!"
A chorus of crickets joins in for the show,
Insects unite, putting on quite the flow.

A beetle complains, "This dance floor is small,
But look at my shell, it's the best of them all!"
The fireflies bling, lighting up with their glow,
"Let's twirl through the meadows, put on a real show!"

So here's to the critters, a whimsical crew,
In this bug ballet, where skies are so blue.
With laughter and buzzing, they twirl and they spin,
An interlude of joy, let the antics begin!

Aroma of the Awakening

Morning dew glistens, oh what a treat,
Daisies and buttercups dance to the beat.
"Who's got the snacks?" yells a hungry bee,
"Sniffing these blooms, there's enough for me!"

In the fragrance of bliss, the blossoms all sway,
A bumblebee trip, in a whimsical way.
"I'm lost in the petals, oh what a tease!"
"Follow my scent, it's a game, if you please!"

Whiffs of sweet nectar waft through the air,
"Enjoy the buffet, but do beware!"
"Watch for the raindrops!" a ladybug shouts,
"Or you'll be soaked, filled with silly doubts!"

As the sun rises high, they enjoy the best brew,
"What a delight! Who knew leaves could woo?"
The aroma around is a tune of pure joy,
In the gardens where laughter meets nature's ploy.

Vows Among the Violets

Two little ants, holding tiny hands,
"Will you be mine, in these flowered lands?"
Under the violets, they giggle and sway,
Making sweet vows in the sun's warm display.

"I promise to share, all crumbs from my lunch,
And dance in the flowers, it's such a great bunch!"
The scent of the petals, wafts through the air,
"Let's make this a bond that no bug can compare!"

A butterfly flutters, overhears the affair,
"Love in the garden? Oh, sweet love is rare!"
"Join us!" they beckon, as they twist and they twirl,
Under the violets, where dreams start to unfurl.

So here's to the vows, in bright blooming light,
Where friendships and giggles take graceful flight.
In a world so bustling, they've found a sweet call,
Amid the sweet nectar, they vow to stand tall.

Dusty Wishes on Soft Breezes

In a garden of giggles, I toss my dreams,
With flowers that dance and tickle my seams.
The bees wear their goggles, buzzing away,
While daisies do ballet, what a funny display.

The sun sneezes pollen, a golden spray,
Tickling my nose in a zany array.
I make a wish on a fluffy old dandelion,
And laugh as the seeds start a raucous rebellion.

The ants in their suits have a meeting at noon,
Debating how many crumbs to bring to the moon.
I join the discussion, wearing a grin,
While the grasshoppers chuckle, as they jump in.

Oh, the whimsy of wishes, on breezes so light,
Makes the world a playground, a comical sight.
With each little giggle that floats on the breeze,
I revel in joy, feeling simply at ease.

In the Company of Butterflies

Fluttering flurries in a trickster hat,
Butterflies giggle, imagine that!
They prance through the tulips, on a daring spree,
Chasing the wind, they're wild and free.

A ladybug joins in, with polka-dot flair,
She twirls with a wink, spreading laughter in air.
They sip on nectar with silly little sips,
While teasing the bumblebees, pulling funny quips.

The caterpillars chuckle, knitting a joke,
As they wiggle and jiggle, they're never broke.
In this garden of whimsy, always a jest,
With each flitting moment, they're giving their best.

Oh, to dance with the flutterers in bright sunny glee,
Life's a carnival ride, come take a selfie!
In the company of laughter and colorful flight,
We sparkle and shine in the warm afternoon light.

Fables of Seasons Passed

Once there was winter, with snowflakes like rocks,
Who slipped on his sled—oh, what a paradox!
He chuckled with spring as they pulled off a prank,
By changing the weather, leaving flowers in the bank.

Then summer showed up, with a sunburned grin,
Said, "Let's throw a party, let the fun begin!"
But autumn came leaping, with leaves like confetti,
And danced through the garden, looking all ready.

Together they laughed, a quirky quartet,
With tales of the past they could never forget.
In hues of the seasons, the merriment flows,
As fables of laughter collect on the rows.

Oh, the joys of the years, all the chuckles we've made,
Through hurry and worry, through sun and through shade.
With nature as witness and humor the key,
These fables of folly are true jubilee.

Moonlit Nectar Dreams

Under the moon, with stars as my cheer,
I dream of sweet nectar, oh what a delight here!
The flowers are giggling, a joyous parade,
While the night gives a wink, in soft silk cascade.

The bats wear their capes, flying in spree,
Chasing shadows and whispers, as happy as can be.
I sip on the moonlight, silver and bright,
While fireflies join in, twinkling their light.

Oh, what a party in the garden so grand,
With critters all laughing in this nighttime band.
The daisies are gossiping, with petals afluff,
And I can't help but chuckle—oh, life's just enough!

As the night whispers secrets and dreams start to bloom,
I frolic through moonlight, dispelling the gloom.
With laughter as nectar, so rich and divine,
In this sweet, silly universe, everything's fine.

Identity in Nature's Palette

In a world of green and gold,
A bee's bold dance, a sight so bold.
He buzzes near a flower's face,
Creating chaos in this space.

The tulips giggle, swaying near,
While daisies mutter, 'What's he here?'
With petals fluffed in lively cheer,
They play their game of hide and peer.

A ladybug struts in bright hue,
With tiny spots, a dandy too.
She winks at ants in lines so straight,
While mocking bees who just can't wait.

As colors clash in joyful blend,
These critters frolic, never end.
Nature's palette, wild and free,
Painting laughs in harmony.

Vibrancy Beneath the Sky

Beneath the sun with hues galore,
A butterfly teases, 'Catch me, soar!'
With wings adorned in polka dots,
He giggles, 'Can you handle plots?'

The grasshoppers jump, a crazy race,
While squirrels twirl in frantic chase.
The clouds above just shake their fluff,
They're laughing hard — enough's enough!

A snail in shell, with graceful pace,
Grumbles slow with a frown on his face.
'Why rush today?' he surely sighs,
While bees get dizzy, buzzing lies.

As blooms erupt in colors bright,
The world spins round, a merry sight.
While shadows dance and laughter grows,
The sky below is all aglow.

The Pulse of Spring's Heart

Spring sings a tune of joyous glee,
While flowers burst, 'Come play with me!'
A rhyming frog croaks in delight,
His concert's scheduled every night.

Frolicsome critters join the party,
A rabbit hops, feeling so hearty.
They munch on greens, a leafy feast,
'Just one more bite!' says giggly beast.

The trees shake hands with breezy flair,
While squirrels exchange glances with care.
They tumble down in laughter bright,
Creating a whirlwind of pure light.

As petals fall like confetti rain,
Laughter echoes, washing the plain.
In springtime's pulse, the joy begins,
Nature's antics — everyone wins!

Fluent Whispers of Nature

In whispers soft, the leaves confide,
With critters sharing secrets wide.
A cheeky chipmunk with a cheeky grin,
'What's silly is how fast we spin?'

The sun peeks out, so round and bright,
Painting shadows in playful light.
While flowers nod, their petals sway,
'It's difficult to keep gray away!'

A witty worm crawls with great pep,
'Uh-oh, I think I've lost my step!'
The butterflies chuckle, teasing near,
'Just wiggle, wiggle! Have no fear!'

With giggles wrapped in nature's charm,
Each creature dances, free from harm.
In this ballet under bright skies,
Laughter lingers, as nature pries.

Underneath the Canopy of Dreams

Beneath the trees where dreams take flight,
Squirrels argue over acorn's might.
The branches shake in laughter's glow,
As bees take tea with a butterfly show.

Frogs in hats croak silly tunes,
While ladybugs dance 'neath glowing moons.
A breeze brings whispers of playful schemes,
Life here is woven of giggles and beams.

In every nook, a jest unfolds,
With mossy carpets and stories told.
Here, the world spins in a comical trance,
Under leafy crowns, it's a joyous dance.

The sky's a canvas, bright and spry,
Where clouds make faces as they float by.
Every rustle is a chuckled delight,
Beneath this canopy, all feels right.

Dancing in Sweet Abundance

In gardens ripe with giddy cheer,
Bees do the tango; have no fear!
Tomatoes blush in sunlit glee,
While strawberries whisper, "Hey, look at me!"

Marigolds twist in a bright ballet,
As radishes tiptoe, come what may.
A pear gets dizzy from laughing too hard,
While cucumbers juggle—no one is scarred.

Lettuce bounces with leafy delight,
The earthworms giggle, oh what a sight!
Every bloom holds a raucous sound,
In this garden of fun, joy is unbound.

With every step, the soil sings,
As nature plays with its little things.
Oh, come and join this frolicking spree,
In sweetness and laughter, one can be free!

The Filigree of Floral Dreams

In a patch of posies, laughter flows,
Petals gossip as the wind blows.
A daisy tells jokes with a wink so bright,
While tulips twirl in sheer delight.

The lilies giggle, donning their crowns,
While violets trade in whimsical frowns.
Sunflowers strike poses, aimed for the sky,
"Look at me!" they boast, oh my, oh my!

Bees wear top hats in this flower show,
And ants march by with a comical flow.
Every sprout wears a whimsical scheme,
In this floral land of dreams, we beam.

As night approaches, crickets begin,
Their chirps are the giggles, a joyous din.
The moon chuckles softly, a silver gleam,
In this world of blooms, life's a funny dream.

Transitory Colors of Life

Colors clash in a vibrant spree,
Where daisies don shades just to tease a bee.
A rainbow slips on its polka-dot shoes,
While butterflies laugh, confused on whose views.

Crayons tossed by a playful breeze,
Paints a picture of squirrels at ease.
A pink sky giggles at day's end,
As fireflies buzz, their light they send.

Every hue has a tale to spin,
In the palette of life, let the fun begin!
So grab a brush, splash joy all around,
In every color, let laughter resound.

The world is a canvas, run wild and free,
Let the shades of joy be all that you see.
In this changing view, we find our delight,
With transitory colors, our spirits take flight.

Embers of Blooming Passion

In gardens bright, where flowers play,
Bees buzz around like kids at a fair.
They flirt with petals, sipping all day,
Wearing bright yellow, like they just don't care.

Each bloom's a dance, a wild soirée,
With pollen confetti flung in the air.
The bees roll their eyes, as if to say,
'Hold my nectar, I'm beyond compare!'

They shimmy and shake, no time for a nap,
Get ready, world, for this buzzing troupe.
In nature's play, there's no room for slack,
Just a vibrant spin, of whimsy and whoop!

A floral fiesta, a sight to be seen,
Where laughter and sweetness bloom in the sun.
So join in the fun, let your heart be keen,
In the garden's embrace, we all can be one.

Cursive Trails in Sunlit Air

Bumblebees scribble in loops and swirls,
On petals soft, where the sunlight sways.
With tiny exclamations, they twirl and whirls,
A dance of delight through the warm summer days.

Sunshine giggles as bees buzz and plot,
Crafting sweet stories on each fragrant bloom.
Like poets in bloom, giving all they've got,
They'll weave a romance, dispelling all gloom.

With each little pollinator throwing a fit,
A plucky parade on the floral parade.
Grab your sun hats, don't you dare sit,
Join this joyride where laughs cascade!

In this buzzing tale, it's love that we find,
So tip your hat and let worries drift low.
For every sweet visit, we're all intertwined,
In cursive trails, where the daisies glow.

A Symphony of Pollinated Hues

Under the sun, colors burst into song,
With bees as our band, playing tunes so bright.
Their wiggly dance, could it be wrong?
In this floral rhapsody, we take flight!

Each petal's a drum, each stamen's a flute,
As nature composes her vibrant display.
With buzzing harmonies that are oh-so-cute,
They paint the air with their sweet ballet.

Stroking the breeze, like skilled violinists,
The flowers swirl with a laugh and a cheer.
Bees throw their hats, with extraordinary twists,
In this symphony, we twirl without fear.

So raise your glass to the buzzing crowd,
For every small pollinator, we sing their praise.
In nature's concert, we find it loud—
A joyful affair that lasts all our days.

Canopy of Sweetness

In a sunlit haven, the bees don't slack,
They wear tiny crowns, oh, what a sight!
With a giggle and jab, they dance with flair,
Creating sweetness, a true delight!

Underneath leaves, like a cozy café,
Buzzy patrons sip nectar with glee.
Clumsy little harlequins, they play all day,
Wobbling on flowers like cups of tea!

The leaves laugh softly, whispering low,
As bees barrel-roll through blossoms and blooms.
In this splendid circus, where giggles overflow,
Every bee's a performer, breaking the gloom.

So come and join in this festival fun,
Where sweetness abounds, and laughter takes flight.
With wings spread wide, beneath the bright sun,
In our canopy world, the bees are just right!

www.ingramcontent.com/pod-product-compliance
Lightning Source LLC
Chambersburg PA
CBHW051634160426
43209CB00004B/639